BEETLE BAILEY:
BEETLE BUGGED

Here's another in the happy series of books based on one of the most famous comic strips in the country. Once again the madcap inmates of Camp Swampy valiantly strive to overcome their own ineptitude — and succeed in delighting us on every page.

Mort Walker again gives us a barrel of laughs in his marvelous cartoons concerning the most unprofessional soldier in the army!

Beetle Bailey Books

beetle bailey
BEETLE BUGGED

Mort Walker

J
JOVE BOOKS, NEW YORK

BEETLE BAILEY: BEETLE BUGGED

A Jove Book / published by arrangement with
King Features Syndicate, Inc.

PRINTING HISTORY
Jove edition / January 1992

ISBN: 0-515-10759-X

Jove Books are published by The Berkley Publishing Group,
200 Madison Avenue, New York, New York 10016.
The name "JOVE" and the "J" logo
are trademarks belonging to Jove Publications, Inc.

PRINTED IN THE UNITED STATES OF AMERICA

10 9 8 7 6 5 4 3 2 1

WHAT A DREAM!
THAT'S THE LAST
TIME I'LL PUT BABY
PEPPERCORNS ON
MY PIZZA

11-24

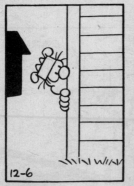

12-6

STRANGE. HOW DO YOU GET OVER HERE WITHOUT RUNNING INTO ME?

MORT WALKER

4-3

4-11